21st Century Skills Library

REAL WORLD MATH: HEALTH AND WELLNESS

DINNER BY THE NUMBERS

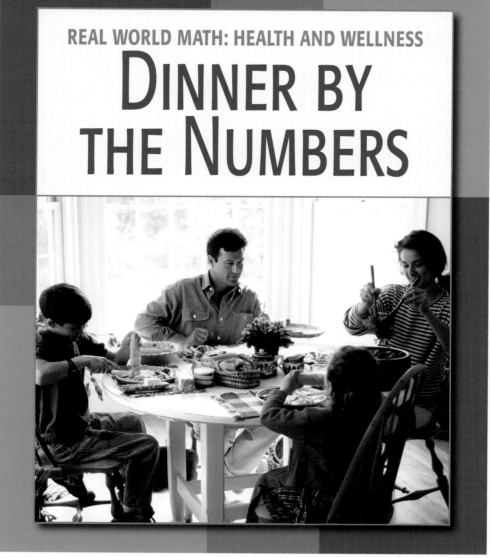

Cecilia Minden

Cherry Lake Publishing
Ann Arbor, Michigan

Published in the United States of America by Cherry Lake Publishing
Ann Arbor, MI
www.cherrylakepublishing.com

Math Adviser: Tonya Walker, MA, Boston University

Nutrition Adviser: Steven Abrams, MD, Professor of Pediatrics, Baylor College of
Medicine, Houston, Texas

Photo Credits: Cover and page 1, © Ariel Skelley/Corbis; page 6, © Charles Gullung/
Zefa/Corbis; page 10, Illustration courtesy of U.S. Department of Agriculture

Library of Congress Cataloging-in-Publication Data
Minden, Cecilia.
 Dinner by the numbers / by Cecilia Minden.
   p. cm. — (Real world math)
 ISBN-13: 978-1-60279-013-1
 ISBN-10: 1-60279-013-2
 1. Family—Juvenile literature. 2. Dinners and dining—Juvenile literature. 3. Cookery—Juvenile
literature. I. Title.
HQ519.M56 2008
306.87—dc22   2007003889

*Cherry Lake Publishing would like to acknowledge the work of
The Partnership for 21st Century Skills.
Please visit www.21stcenturyskills.org for more information.*

TABLE OF CONTENTS

CHAPTER ONE

AROUND THE DINNER TABLE

Everyone can lend a hand to help get dinner ready.

Dad is carving a turkey. Mom is steaming fresh vegetables. Your brother is

slicing a loaf of freshly baked bread, and your sister is mixing a fruit salad. It's

your job to set the table and pour everyone a tall glass of cold milk or water.

Family meals give kids and parents time together and a chance to talk and listen to one another. Studies show that kids in families who share meals eat more vegetables and fruits. They choose fewer unhealthy snacks. They are also less likely to drink alcohol, smoke, or abuse drugs.

Everyone can help plan and cook a healthy, tasty family dinner. Once you take your place at the dinner table, interesting conversations are sure to follow. You can ask questions, tell stories, and learn about each other's day. Family dinners are also a time to practice good table manners.

In 2001, the National Center on Addiction and Substance Abuse at Columbia University in New York City, New York, created Family Day—A Day to Eat Dinner with Your Children. The goal is to encourage families to dine together. Family Day is celebrated on the fourth Monday in September.

Many families have special dinnertime **rituals**. Some people begin the

meal with a prayer. Others discuss current events or a story they heard

on the news. Some families take turns asking thoughtful questions, such

as "What country would you like to visit?" or "What was the best part of

your day?"

Family rituals should include good table manners. They say a lot

about who you are. They reflect how you want to be treated. Good

*Dinnertime gives family members a chance
to share food and conversation.*

manners show respect for other people at the table. Most table manners are easy to remember and go a long way toward creating a relaxed, pleasant atmosphere.

Wait until everyone is seated before eating. Take a moment to thank the cook or anyone who played an important role in preparing the meal. Wait your turn to speak. Be considerate of other people's ideas. Let the voices you hear be your family's and not the TV, radio, or phone. Additional important table manners include:

- Wash your hands both before and after a meal.

- Keep your napkin on your lap.

- Pass items rather than grabbing them.

- Keep your mouth closed when chewing food.

- Wait until everyone has finished before leaving the table.

A family dinner gives everyone a chance to reconnect. It is a chance to refuel with **nutritious** food at the end of the day. It is a special time because it allows your loved ones to catch up with one another over a good meal.

Chicken, vegetables, and potatoes can all be part of a healthy dinner.

CHAPTER TWO

MAKE THE MEAL HAPPEN!

Family meals don't just happen. Preparing a balanced and delicious dinner for everyone takes planning and work. Give each family member a specific job. This makes it easier and quicker to get both the food and the table ready. You will have more time to enjoy dinner and one another's company. Suggested tasks include:

• Setting the table with dishes, silverware, napkins, and glasses

• Washing fresh fruits and vegetables

• Grating cheese

• Putting food in serving dishes on the table

• Clearing the table after dinner

• Putting any leftover food back in the refrigerator or freezer

Each color in the food pyramid represents a a different food group. Visit www.MyPyramid.gov to learn more about the food groups and planning healthy meals.

- Washing dishes, pots, pans, silverware, and other cooking utensils

- Sweeping the kitchen and dining area

- Wiping off any surfaces that were used to prepare food

Wondering what to serve for your family meal? Try to keep it simple. This is a night for relaxation and quality time together. Create a list of favorite family dishes. Who does most of the cooking at your home? That person will be a big help in making sure the foods needed for the meal are in the house. Use www.MyPyramid.gov to help you make healthy choices. Include grains, vegetables, fruits, milk, and meat or beans at each meal. You may also use some oil, but you only need a little. Be certain everyone has a job to do so no one feels left out.

21st Century Content

Visit MyPyramid.gov to learn more about how to choose healthy meals. The food pyramid there places foods in the following categories: grains, vegetables, fruits, milk, meat and beans, and oils.

Grains are foods made from wheat, rice, oats, barley, and other whole grains. Vegetables can be fresh, frozen, canned, or dried. Whole fruits or 100 percent fruit juice are a part of the fruit group. Milk and products made from milk, such as yogurt and cheese, are in the milk group. Foods in the meat and bean group include meat (beef and pork, for example), **poultry**, fish, nuts, eggs, and beans (including black, kidney, and navy beans). The oils category features liquid oils such as olive and canola oil, solid fats such as butter, and other foods high in fat content such as mayonnaise and salad dressings.

The Web site also includes information on serving sizes and how many servings you need from each food group every day.

Here are some dinner menu ideas you might want to try:

- Whole grain pizza crust topped with low-fat mozzarella cheese and vegetables, fruit salad, and low-fat milk

- Baked chicken, steamed vegetables, whole grain rolls, quick-cooking brown rice, and milkshakes made of frozen strawberries and low-fat milk

- Lean roast beef, baked sweet potatoes with low-fat margarine, green salad with low-fat dressing, frozen yogurt, and apple juice

Remember, low-fat and whole grain foods are an important part of a healthy diet. On the other hand, it's not bad for you to occasionally enjoy a cheeseburger and fries or a slice of chocolate cake. The key to eating treats that are higher in fat and **calories** is to only have them once in a while.

CHAPTER THREE

Do the Math:
A Balanced Meal

As you plan your family dinner, consider all the different food

categories you need to include, as well as healthy serving sizes.

Comparing serving sizes to common objects you can easily visualize in

your head might help. For example, 1 cup of potatoes, pasta, or rice is

Healthy portions of colorful fruits and vegetables
should be part of every dinner.

That's a lot of pasta! Remember to watch your portion sizes.

about the size of a tennis ball. A 3-ounce (85-gram) serving of meat is

about the size of a deck of cards. A medium piece of fruit or 1 cup of

leafy green vegetables is about the size of a baseball. A 1.5-ounce (42.5-g) serving of cheese is about the size of four stacked dice. And 1 teaspoon (5 milliliters) of oil is about the size of the tip of your thumb.

When you make your selections, be aware that a 9- to 13-year-old needs about 5 to 6 ounces (142 to 170 g) of grain, 2 to 2.5 cups of vegetables, 1.5 cups of fruit, 3 cups (750 ml) of milk (or 3 servings of other foods found in the milk group), 5 ounces (142 g) of meat (or the equivalent in other protein-rich foods if you do not eat meat), and 5 teaspoons (25 ml) of fat each day. These should be spread throughout the day, typically in three meals and one or two snacks.

21st Century Content

The energy available in food is measured in calories. Experts recommend that a 10- to 12-year-old of average size should consume about 2,000 calories a day. The exact number depends on how active you are. A very active person burns more calories, while someone who is not as physically active burns less. If you eat more calories than your body uses in a day, the extra energy is stored as fat. In other words, you will gain weight.

REAL WORLD MATH CHALLENGE

Mazie is making dinner for her family. She is serving pasta with **marinara** sauce, turkey meatballs, garlic bread, mixed greens salad with dressing, and ice water.

Which food groups are represented in her dinner?

How many food groups are represented overall?

Which food groups are missing?

Each person's dinner has the following **portion** sizes and calorie counts:

- 1 cup pasta—240 calories
- 1/2 cup marinara sauce—50 calories
- 2 turkey meatballs—120 calories
- 1 piece of garlic bread—120 calories
- 2 cups mixed greens salad—50 calories
- 2 tablespoons (30 ml) low-fat dressing—20 calories
- 1 cup ice water—0 calories

What is the total number of calories for one person's meal?

Mazie's older brother adds another 1/2 cup sauce, two more meatballs, and another slice of bread.

What is his calorie count?

How would Mazie's total calories for the meal change if she skips the bread and adds a milkshake made of 3/4 cup low-fat milk (100 calories) and 3/4 cup fresh strawberries (20 calories)?

How many food groups will be represented if Mazie chooses this option?

(Turn to page 29 for the answers)

CHAPTER FOUR

DO THE MATH:
SPECIAL OCCASIONS

Imagine how much food a restaurant needs in order to plan meals. A busy

restaurant might use 200 loaves of bread and 10 pounds (4.5 kilograms) of

cheese in just one day. A single family doesn't normally eat that much, but

A chef needs to estimate how many customers will visit the restaurant each day and prepare enough food for all of them.

Even young family members can help prepare meals.

there are times when you need to increase

the amounts of various ingredients in a

favorite recipe. You might find yourself in this

situation as you prepare for a holiday dinner

or a meal during a big sports game. Your

math skills are essential in helping you feed a

crowd of hungry people.

Read your recipe carefully. Look closely

at the portion size and the number of people

the recipe serves. Recipes usually feed an

even number such as four, six, or eight. How

many people will be at your dinner? Try to

figure an amount closest to that number. If

What do you think might happen
if you don't use the proper
amounts of each ingredient in
a recipe? How can you be
certain to use the most accurate
measurements when cooking?
Follow these tips to make sure
your recipes turn out just right:

After pouring liquid in the
measuring cup, place it on a shelf
at eye level. This will help you
view how the ingredients hit the
markings more clearly.

Spoon the flour and sugar
into a measuring cup instead of
scooping the cup into a canister of
either ingredient. This will prevent
air pockets from forming.

Use a small knife to smooth off
the top of measuring spoons. This
will help you get the exact amount
of the ingredient you need.

When using a food scale, don't
forget to weigh the container first
and, with the container on the
scale, reset the scale to zero. You
just want to weigh the food—not
the container!

you have seven guests and the recipe is for four, you can simply multiply each ingredient by two. If the recipe is for eight and you have four guests, then you divide each ingredient by two.

Knowing how to work with fractions is a big help when increasing or decreasing a recipe. And remember, it is generally better to have a little extra when serving guests so you can be sure everyone has enough to eat. You can always enjoy the leftovers for lunch the following day!

REAL WORLD MATH CHALLENGE

Dominic is having eight friends over for dinner. He is making chili, and the recipe serves six.

Including himself, how many people does Dominic need to cook for?

What number should he multiply the amounts in the recipe by to prepare enough servings?

If the original recipe requires 2 cups of water, how much water will he need when cooking for his guests?

(Turn to page 29 for the answers)

(Turn to page 29 for the answers)

Leftover chili can be stored in the freezer. Just reheat it for a quick meal on a day when there is no time to cook.

REAL WORLD MATH CHALLENGE

Ella's aunt, uncle, and two cousins are coming for dinner. Ella plans on serving fruit salad. The original recipe serves four people and includes the following ingredients:

1/2 cantaloupe

1 1/2 large bananas

1/2 honeydew melon

1/4 teaspoon (1.2 ml) salt

Ella has to double the recipe. How much of each ingredient does she need?

(Turn to page 29 for the answers)

CHAPTER FIVE

WINNING DINNERTIME STRATEGIES

Read restaurant menus carefully to find meals that include foods from all of the food groups.

Sometimes it just isn't realistic for everyone to be home in time to cook a meal together. With a little creativity, however, you can still enjoy a healthy family dinner.

It is possible to eat balanced meals at restaurants. Look for foods that

are labeled "heart healthy" or "low-fat." Fresh or steamed vegetables, fresh

fruit, and whole grain breads are good selections. Try to choose baked or

Salads are a healthy choice found on most restaurant menus.

Milk is a healthier drink choice than sugary sodas.

broiled meat or fish. Ask for low-fat milk, 100 percent juice, or water instead of a sugar-filled soft drink. Don't make a habit of eating foods that are fried or covered in a rich sauce. It's okay to eat these things occasionally.

REAL WORLD MATH CHALLENGE

Kevin is eating dinner at Captain Chris Seafood. He orders fish, a mixed greens salad, and a baked potato. The server presents Kevin with four choices: 1) Does he want his fish baked or fried? 2) What kind of dressing does he want on his salad? 3) What topping does he want on his baked potato? 4) What does he want to drink with his meal?

Meal #1: Fried fish (210 calories), mixed greens salad with blue cheese dressing (190 calories), a baked potato with butter, sour cream, and bacon bits (380 calories), and a medium soda (210 calories)

Meal #2: Baked fish (120 calories), a mixed greens salad with low-fat Italian dressing (93 calories), a baked potato with butter (204 calories), and a glass of low-fat chocolate milk (170 calories)

Total up each of Kevin's choices. How many calories does each meal have? What is the difference in calories between the two meals?

(Turn to page 29 for the answers)

How about using your leadership skills to influence your family's restaurant meal choices? Many restaurants have their own Web sites. Check out your favorite restaurant's site to see if they list the nutritional information for their food. Pay particular attention to entries that deal with calories, fat content, and sugar content. Jot down the menu items that are low in calories, fat, and sugar. Use your list as a guide and get a conversation started about making healthier meal choices. Then set an example by choosing healthy menu options. You never know, everyone else might follow your lead!

Add fresh vegetables to a plain cheese pizza for a quick and tasty meal.

What about the times you can't sit down at a restaurant and don't

have time to cook? There are several ways to make take-out food a

healthy choice. A plain cheese pizza can be improved at home with extra vegetables. Chicken nuggets, sliced apples, and low-fat milk (460 calories) are a better choice than a double cheeseburger, small fries, and a soft drink (830 calories). When at the deli, choose lean meats or vegetable dishes. You can add a fresh salad and whole grain rolls at home.

Eating dinner picnic style can make even simple sandwiches special!

There are many ways to enjoy nutritious food in the company of your family. You can cook at home, dine at a fancy restaurant, or get take-out food. These meals don't always have to be dinners either. A leisurely weekend breakfast or lunch also gives everyone a chance to be together. You can even choose a group activity when you finish eating. How about taking a long walk or bike ride together? It doesn't matter if it's morning, noon, or night, it's always good to make healthful decisions and fit in some quality time with your family.

REAL WORLD MATH CHALLENGE ANSWERS

Chapter Three

Page 15

Mazie's dinner features four food groups: grains, vegetables, meat, and oils. The milk and fruit groups are not represented.

The total number of calories for each person's meal is 600.

240 + 50 + 120 + 120 + 50 + 20 + 0 = 600 calories

Mazie's older brother's calorie count is 890 calories.

600 + 50 + 120 + 120 = 890 calories

If Mazie skips the bread and adds the milkshake to her meal, her calorie count will be 600 calories.

[600 − 120 = 480] + 100 + 20 = 600 total calories

If Mazie chooses this meal option, all six food groups—including milk and fruits—will be represented.

Chapter Four

Page 20

Dominic needs to cook for 9 people.

8 + 1 = 9

To prepare enough servings, Dominic has to multiply the amounts by 1.5.

9 ÷ 6 = 1.5

Dominic will need 3 cups of water when cooking for his guests.

2 cups x 1.5 = 3 cups

Page 21

If Ella doubles the recipe she will need 1 cantaloupe (1/2 x 2 = 1), 3 bananas (1½ x 2 = 3), and 1 honeydew melon (1/2 x 2 = 1), and ½ teaspoon (2.4 ml) salt (1/4 x 2 = ½).

Chapter Five

Page 25

Meal #1 contains 990 calories.

210 + 190 + 380 + 210 = 990

Meal #2 has 587 calories.

120 + 93 + 204 + 170 = 587

Meal #2 has 403 less calories than Meal #1.

990 − 587 = 403

Glossary

bacteria (bak-TIR-ee-uh) tiny organisms often found on raw or unwashed foods that can lead to illness in people who eat them

calories (KAL-uh-reez) the measurement of the amount of energy available to your body in the food you eat

marinara (mehr-uh-NEHR-uh) a sauce made with tomatoes and a variety of spices

nutritious (new-TRISH-uss) adding value to one's diet by contributing to health or growth

portion (POR-shuhn) a part or share of something; enough of one kind of food to serve someone at a meal

poultry (POHL-tree) birds that are raised for their meat and eggs; chickens, turkeys, ducks, and geese are poultry

rituals (RIH-choo-uhlz) customs or traditions

utensils (yoo-TEN-suhlz) tools used for eating or preparing food

FOR MORE INFORMATION

Books

Creech, Sharon, and Chris Raschka (illustrator). *Granny Torrelli Makes Soup*. New York: Joanna Cotler Books, 2003.

Lagasse, Emeril, Charles Yuen (illustrator). *Emeril's There's a Chef in My Family! Recipes to Get Everybody Cooking*. New York: HarperCollins Publishers, 2004.

Pierson, Stephanie. *Vegetables Rock! A Complete Guide for Teenage Vegetarians*. New York: Bantam Books, 1999.

Web Sites

Family Education—Family Dinners: The Recipe for Connectedness
life.familyeducation.com/dinner/family-time/29528.html?detoured=1
Tips for how to get the most out of family mealtimes and links to family-friendly recipes

U.S. Department of Agriculture—MyPyramid.gov
www.mypyramid.gov/
Information about the food groups and preparing balanced meals

INDEX

ABOUT THE AUTHOR

Cecilia Minden, PhD, is a literacy consultant and the author of many books for children. She is the former director of the Language and Literacy Program at Harvard Graduate School of Education in Cambridge, Massachusetts. She would like to thank fifth-grade math teacher Beth Rottinghaus for her help with the Real World Math Challenges. Cecilia lives with her family in North Carolina.